How To Store Your Garden Produce

The key to self-sufficiency

Piers Warren

with illustrations by Chris Winn

Green Books

Published by
Green Books
Foxhole, Dartington,
Totnes, Devon TQ9 6EB
www.greenbooks.co.uk

First published 2002 by Wildeye
This edition published March 2003, reprinted October 2003

Printed by Bell & Bain Ltd, Glasgow

ISBN 1 903998 25 5

This book is dedicated to
Monica
Who eats the veg I store!

.

Many thanks to
Chris Winn
Roland Clare
John Yeoman
Morgan West

Contents

Introduction   9

Part One: The Methods

General Guidelines   17
Freezing   18
Clamping   25
Hanging   26
Dry Storage   27
Drying   28
Bottling   29
Pickles and Chutneys   31
Jams   33
Fermenting   35

Part Two: The Produce

Apples   39
Artichokes   41
Asparagus   42
Aubergines   43
Beans – Broad   44
Beans – French   45
Beans – Runner   46
Beetroot   47
Blackberries   48
Black Currants (plus Red and White Currants)   49
Broccoli (and Calabrese)   51

Contents (continued)

Brussels Sprouts   52
Cabbages   53
Carrots   54
Cauliflower   55
Celeriac   56
Celery   57
Cherries   58
Chicory   59
Cucumbers   60
Endive   61
Fennel   62
Garlic   63
Gooseberries   64
Grapes   66
Herbs   67
Kale   69
Kohlrabi   70
Leeks   71
Lettuces   72
Marrows (Courgettes, Squashes, Pumpkins)   73
Mushrooms   75
Okra   76
Onions   77
Parsnips   78
Peas   80
Peaches (plus Apricots and Nectarines)   81

Contents (continued)

Pears   82

Peppers (Capsicum and Chilli)   84

Plums (plus Damsons and Greengages)   85

Potatoes   87

Radishes   88

Raspberries (plus Loganberries)   89

Rhubarb   91

Salsify (plus Scorzonera)   92

Spinach   93

Strawberries   94

Swedes   95

Sweet corn   96

Tomatoes   97

Turnips   99

About the Author   100

About the Illustrator   101

Introduction

Why is storing your garden produce the key to self-sufficiency?

Because with less than an acre of garden you can grow enough produce to feed a family of four for a year. But since much of the produce will become ready at the same time – in the summer – most of it will go to waste without proper storage, and you'll be off to the supermarket again…

I've always been obsessed with the idea of self-sufficiency, and have always hated waste, so as a keen vegetable grower it was only natural that I explored the overlooked art of storage.

To some extent is it a lost art. These days you can go to the supermarket any day of the week and buy produce from many different countries.

Imagine being told that the lettuces were all sold out – try again in six months!

In the past, effective storage was a matter of life and death. If your potatoes rotted your family would go hungry, possibly even starve.

I have also always had a problem buying vegetables or fruit that have been flown half way round the world when I had been growing them myself only a few months earlier.

Plus there are so many other benefits from eating your own produce year round:

1. A HUGE sense of satisfaction – of self-reliance – that you can personally meet the most important need of your family.

2. Home-grown fruit and vegetables are far cheaper than shop-bought (if not free) – and you will have healthy exercise growing them!

3. What are you eating? You have little chance of knowing what chemicals or genetic modification have been used on produce you buy from a shop. At least you know what's happened to your own fruit and veg – and if you're an organic gardener like me (which I thoroughly recommend), you'll know your produce couldn't be safer.

4. Eating food you have produced in your own garden is the most environmentally sound way of doing things. No unnecessary packaging, no transport pollution, no encouragement of vast monocrops and so on.

5. Pleasure! Some storage activities – stringing onions, making cider, concocting chutneys – are pleasurable in themselves, and the end products are definitely for enjoyment!

Why do we need special methods in the first place?

When keeping fresh food for any length of time we have four main enemies: enzymes, bacteria, yeasts and fungi.

Enzymes are proteins naturally found in all fresh produce which control various processes: some of them help break down food as we digest it. They can work pretty quickly: for example they are responsible for apples turning rapidly brown when cut. Enzymes can spoil food soon after harvesting, so our aim must be to halt their action. Extreme heat stops the enzymes working permanently, as is the case in bottling. Extreme cold stops them working temporarily – as in freezing.

Bacteria are micro-organisms which can multiply rapidly. They are the main causes of food poisoning – either by producing toxins (e.g. causing botulism), or by being poisonous themselves. Contamination can come from anywhere – soil, hands, apparently clean jars etc. – so the key is to halt or slow their growth. This can be done by killing them with extreme heat, or slowing their activity with cold or acid conditions, as in pickling.

Yeasts are also microscopic but are not dangerous like bacteria. Of course they can be our friends when fermenting sugar to make cider, wine and beer. In terms of spoilage they are most often responsible for fermenting jams. As they are destroyed by heat, they must have contaminated the jam after potting. Their activity is slowed down by cold, which is why it is a good idea to keep opened jams in the fridge.

Fungi produce minuscule spores that are in the air all around us, so any uncovered food will sooner or later be infected. As the fungal growth develops the food will appear mouldy and will be unfit for consumption, although rarely dangerous. Freezing will stop fungal growth, but equally important are methods to stop spores reaching the food in the first place: burying harvested carrots in sand for example.

Storage and preservation techniques fight these enemies mainly by using heat, cold, acid, or by simply creating conditions where spoilage is less likely.

Note that although there are some methods – such as drying and bottling – that may render food safe to eat for years, your aim should be to store food only until the next season's fresh produce is available. This ensures you are eating the highest quality stored food at all times.

So, how can this book help you?

Part One looks at the various storage methods in general. Many of these are applicable to a range of produce. Start here to get a good background of the methods available. It is true that some of the methods would be more accurately defined as preservation rather than storage – making jam for example – but it is useful to have the full range of possibilities in front of you when deciding what to do with your mountain of raspberries!

Part Two is more of a reference section, which lists most plant produce grown commonly in gardens and allotments. For each one the most appropriate methods are listed with specific advice.

Some methods, such as the clamping of roots, have been passed through many generations. Others, such as freezing, are relatively new. And there are those which are continually developing – invent a new chutney, for example, and you have added to the armoury of storage methods!

Part One

The Methods

General Guidelines

1. Harvest produce for storage in its peak condition.

2. Handle produce carefully: bruised fruit and vegetables will rot quickly.

3. Some varieties store better than others – if you are growing some crops for storage, research your varieties first.

4. Do not store near strong smelling substances or hazardous chemicals (often a problem when storing in a garage or garden shed). Creosote flavoured potatoes are not my favourite.

5. Check your stored produced regularly, and remove any that are rotting to reduce the chance of it spreading.

6. Plan what you store (and therefore grow) according to your family's tastes. There's little point in storing 20 pumpkins if your family is bored with them after eating 2 or 3.

7. Don't make the mistake of eating year-old beans from the freezer while fresh ones are ready in the garden. The priority is always to EAT the freshest produce while fresh, then store the excess. If you have a freezer full of year old beans you have simply grown too many beans!

Freezing

We start with freezing because it is the one method that has relatively recently revolutionised the storage of fruit and vegetables for many households. It's also quick, easy, and very effective.

Freezing halts, or at least dramatically slows down, the action of enzymes (which break down vitamins for example) occurring from the moment food is harvested. So, food frozen shortly after picking will be among the healthiest of stored produce. The cold also stops micro-organisms from growing and spreading. Many fruit and vegetables can be stored in the deep-freeze for up to 12 months, giving you year-round access to home-grown goodness.

If you're serious about storage you will soon find you need a chest freezer (or two)! For the average home the ideal combination would be to have an upright fridge-freezer in the kitchen, where you can store small amounts for quick access, and then a chest (or upright) freezer in a garage, utility room etc., for the bulk of your frozen produce.

Let's look at a few general rules:

1. Freeze food as quickly as possible after harvesting – some, like peas and sweet corn for example, will start to lose their sweetness within minutes of being picked. Timing is everything!

2. Freeze your best. If you don't like tough, stringy beans you won't like them after they've been frozen either. Freeze young and tender and perfect, not forgetting to EAT as much fresh as you want first of course!

3. Pack food in appropriate plastic bags or containers. This is partly to exclude as much air as possible, since air dries out the food and slows freezing. Save old ice cream containers, margarine tubs and yoghurt pots for use in the freezer.

4. Label your packages. What is that bag of green mush that's been sitting there for a year?! It's best to write on the bag or container with a waterproof pen, mentioning what it is and the date of freezing.

5. When food is frozen after blanching (or cooking) make sure it is completely cool before putting it in the freezer.

6. Do not place unfrozen food against deep frozen packages – it will start to thaw and so the frozen food will deteriorate. Some freezers have a rack for placing the new food on as it freezes.

7. If you are freezing liquids such as fruit juices, remember they will expand as they freeze. So freeze in plastic bags inside old drinks cartons – once frozen, the blocks can be stacked with no wastage of space. Or freeze in empty (and well cleaned) plastic milk containers, but leave a space at the top for expansion.

8. Some freezers have a fast-freeze button which overrides the thermostat and keeps the temperature low while new additions are freezing. Don't forget to switch this off after a few hours (depending on the amount of unfrozen food added). The freezer will then return to the normal temperature of -18°C.

9. Organise your freezer. You may find coloured bags or boxes help you find the right items quickly. Rotate your stock – a 3 year-old bag of sprouts that you will never eat is a waste of space. You might even find it useful to keep a list of what is in the freezer with dates, and then cross items off as you use them.

10. Cook, or eat, food as soon as possible after it comes out of the freezer, as the spoiling enzymes will start working again straight away (as well as any bacteria or fungi that may have contaminated the food). Vegetables can generally be cooked from frozen, while fruits are better left to thaw slowly in the fridge.

Defrosting the freezer

The best time to do this is in the spring when the freezer should be at its emptiest, having been raided all winter.

First, empty the contents (throwing away anything too old or unwanted on the compost heap) and make a pile of the frozen food in cool boxes or on newspaper on the floor. Cover this pile with paper, towels, blankets – anything to insulate it.

Switch the freezer off, place a wad of newspaper inside, in the bottom, and a large pan of hot water on top of the paper. Close the lid and leave for thirty minutes. This may be long enough but if there is still a lot of ice inside put in a fresh pan of hot water and leave for another twenty minutes or so.

When all the ice has gone, soak up the water and give the freezer a good clean inside. Then close the lid, switch on, and after fifteen minutes replace the food.

Open-freezing

Some fruit and vegetables (e.g. broccoli) stick together in a lump when frozen, making it difficult to remove small portions later without

smashing the lump to green shrapnel.

The solution is 'open-freezing'. Simply lay the food out on a baking sheet so that the individual pieces are not touching, and place this in the freezer. When frozen, the food can be placed in a bag or container to exclude as much air as possible. Now when you come to use the frozen food it should be suitably loose.

Blanching

Recommended for nearly all vegetables, blanching is the immersing of the fresh vegetables in boiling water for a minute or two immediately before freezing. The reason for doing this is to slow down the enzymes which cause the food to deteriorate, even while frozen. This improves the colour, flavour and nutritional value of the food.

As a rule of thumb, blanch small pieces of vegetables (e.g. peas, beans) for 1 minute, and larger pieces (e.g. cauliflower, parsnips) for 2 minutes. A few vegetables need longer blanching and these are detailed in Part Two.

Usually I find I am blanching fairly large quantities of harvested crops at the same time. The best method I have found is to have two large pans on the hob, one filled with water and brought to the boil. In the sink have a large bowl or two of cold water ready.

Place the first batch of vegetables (say 500 g) in the hot water, bring back to the boil, and then time for the relevant number of minutes. Then carefully pour through a colander into the second pan, and put that on the hot plate in place of the first. Tip the vegetables from the colander into a bowl of cold water and swirl around to cool quickly. When the water (now in the second pan) returns to the boil add the next batch of vegetables, boil and time as before. While this is happening, tip the first batch of vegetables in the cold water through another colander and refill the bowl with cold water ready to cool the next lot. You may find a wire basket – such as a chip basket – useful for dipping the food into the pan and the cold water without the need for tipping.

After a while you will develop a good routine for this. The main things to be careful with are not to boil the vegetables for too long, to cool them quickly after blanching, and to ensure they are completely cool before bagging and freezing.

Cooked Produce

Of course some fruit and vegetables can be frozen after they have been cooked, for example new potatoes, tomato purée, stewed apples or plums. Again, these are detailed in Part Two where relevant.

Clamping

Clamping is a simple method for storing a large quantity of root vegetables outside. It's great where indoor storage space is limited but not so good if you have hard frosts. Basically it is a pile, with straw and earth on top! The following guidelines will help your clamped roots store longer:

1. Choose a site on a piece of ground unlikely to become waterlogged.

2. Harvest your root crops and allow to dry on the surface of the soil for a couple of hours.

3. To build the clamp start with a good layer of straw or bracken, and on top of this pile up your potatoes or other roots in a pyramid shape.

4. Cover the pile with a layer of straw or bracken and leave to sweat for a day or two (the evaporation of excess moisture).

5. Cover the straw with a layer of dryish earth about 15 cm thick, making sure there are small tunnels of straw sticking through the earth along the bottom and chimneys along the top to allow for air circulation. Pat the earth flat with a spade to form a smooth, steep-sided pyramid that rain will easily run off.

Make a series of smaller clamps rather than one enormous one – when you want a handful of potatoes it's not easy to burrow into a clamp and then rebuild it. Better to dismantle a small clamp and bring a sackful of spuds into a shed or garage for easy access until the next clamp is needed.

Hanging

Mainly used for onions and squashes. The best place to hang vegetables for storage is in a dry cool airy place which won't be hit by hard frosts. A stone or brick outbuilding is ideal as long as it isn't too damp. A garage might be OK as long as it doesn't smell of petrol or oil, but beware of thin wooden sheds which frost can penetrate. And certainly not the warm kitchen, no matter how attractive strings of onions may look!

Squashes such as marrows and pumpkins can be hung in nets – just make sure the fruits are not touching each other. Save any netting or net bags for this purpose, such as the net sacks that stock-feed carrots often come in.

Netting bags (or even tights) can be used for hanging onions or garlic, but just aren't as picturesque as stringing. Before you string onions make sure that they have dried adequately. Fork them up on a sunny day and leave to dry out on the soil surface complete with stalks.

To start your string take four onions and tie the stalks together, then tie the knotted stalks to a piece of string. Hang this from the roof of your store and then add further onions, one at a time, by tying their stalks around the string and sliding them down to meet the others. Don't add so many that the string breaks!

Dry Storage

Some roots such as carrots, parsnips and beetroots can be stored in sand or sawdust (or a peat substitute). The important points are:

1. Use sand that is only just moist. If too wet, prepare in advance by spreading out your sand on a plastic sheet in the hot sun in the summer, then keep in plastic sacks under cover until needed.

2. Make layers of sand and roots (unwashed but with excess soil gently brushed off) in containers such as barrels, crates, deep seed trays, making sure the roots don't touch each other.

3. Store the containers in a dry, frost-free place. If they are large, fill them in situ – have you ever tried to lift a barrel full of sand?

Fruits such as apples and pears can be stored on shelves or in boxes. They need a slightly different environment in that they like the air to be a little moist. A cool dark outhouse is ideal – you can occasionally wet the floor to keep the humidity up.

Choose only perfect unblemished specimens for dry storage. The fruit should not be touching, so either space them apart or wrap individually in paper – this stops the rotting fungi and bacteria spreading from one to another. Greaseproof paper is good, but even newspaper is better than nothing. If you have hundreds of apples you may not have the patience for wrapping each one, so why not just wrap a few crates-worth for the longest storage – you should still be eating them next spring. Note that the fruit that ripens late in the season will keep better, and some varieties, such as Cox's and Bramley's, keep better than others.

Drying

Enzymes, bacteria, yeasts and fungi all require moisture, so drying food is effective at preventing the action of all of them. Although once popular, drying (and salting) can be a time-consuming business, and not convenient for large quantities, so it has largely been replaced by freezing.

Beans, peas and sweet corn used to be dried every autumn by many country families for winter use, but a pea freshly cooked from the freezer will be more tender and flavoursome and will contain more vitamins. These days drying is mainly used for storing herbs and mushrooms.

A warm, dry place is needed for drying. An airing cupboard may do but will take a few days; a warm oven (45°–55°C) will take a few hours. Herbs can be hung in bunches or laid out on a baking sheet. Apples can also be dried by slicing thinly, threading on a string, and hanging over the stove or in a warm oven for a few hours. Once dried the produce must be stored in air-tight jars.

Beans and peas are best dried by leaving the pods on the plants until they have turned yellow, then cut the plant at ground level and hang indoors to dry completely. When the pods have become brittle, shell them and leave on trays for a few days. Then store in a cool dry place in air-tight containers.

Bottling

Bottling is another dying art due to the arrival of freezers; it used to be one of the most popular storage methods but is now usually reserved for speciality fruits.

The idea is that the food in the bottles, or jars, is heated to a high-enough temperature, for a certain time, to kill the bacteria, yeasts and fungi, and stop enzyme activity. As the jars are sealed at heat, there should be no re-introduction of spoiling micro-organisms.

You need special strong bottling jars – either screw-topped or clip jars, both of which use rubber rings for sealing. Fruit can be bottled in water but a sugar syrup gives better colour and flavour (generally about 400 g sugar per litre of water).

The bottles can either be heated in a large pan of water or in the oven. Whichever method you use it is important to reach the right temperature for the right amount of time – these are detailed in Part Two.

If using a large pan, first fill the jars with fruit, then with hot (60°C) syrup. Put the lids on the jars (fasten clips but do not tighten screw-tops), place in the pan and completely cover with warm water. Heat the water and simmer for the required amount of time. Then remove the jars, screw the lids tight, and leave to cool.

If using the oven method, first heat it to 150°C. Fill the jars with fruit and then boiling syrup, and then fit the lids (but not the metal screw bands – heat these separately in the oven). Place the jars in the oven for the required amount of time, then remove and screw the hot bands on tightly – you'll need gloves for this! Leave the jars to cool.

In either case, after cooling, the screw-tops should be loosened slightly for storage or they may be impossible to remove later.

Pickles and Chutneys

The difference between pickles and chutneys is that pickles are usually pieces of vegetables or fruit stored in vinegar, whereas chutneys are mixtures of chopped vegetables and fruits cooked in vinegar. So good old Branston pickle is better described as chutney! In either case it is the acid conditions produced by the vinegar which inhibit the actions of spoiling micro-organisms.

Most pickles and chutneys improve in flavour if left to mature for a few months.

Pickles

1. Choose young, unblemished vegetables, and clean and cut to suitable size while fresh.

2. Soak the vegetables in brine (100 g of salt dissolved in each litre of water), generally for 24 hours. This draws some water out of the vegetables, which improves their preservation. Alternatively they may be packed in salt for a day. Others, such as beetroot, may be cooked before pickling.

3. Pack the vegetables in jars and cover with vinegar by 1 cm or more.

4. Put lids on tightly, as the acid vinegar will corrode metal, make sure that metal lids are either plastic-coated, or use wax paper under the lid.

A variety of vinegars can be used for pickling: malt, wine or cider. Pickling vinegar is usually malt vinegar which has spices added. You can make your own by steeping whole spices in vinegar for a month or so before pickling, or add mustard seeds and peppercorns (or even dried chilli peppers) to the jars.

Chutneys are for experimenters! All sorts of combinations of fruit and vegetables make great chutneys and a few guideline recipes are given in Part Two.

The basics are:

1. Finely chop all the fruit and vegetables. Onions and spices nearly always feature in chutneys; other common additions are apple, raisins and tomatoes.

2. Place in a large pan (NOT iron or copper) with salt, sugar, vinegar and spices of your choice. For each 4 kg of fruit/vegetable, add about 20 g salt, 400 g sugar and 500 ml–1 litre vinegar.

3. Simmer until tender: 30 minutes to 3 hours depending on ingredients.

4. Sterilise jars by boiling in water for ten minutes, or placing in an oven at 160°C for at least ten minutes. Spoon the chutney into the sterile jars while hot, put lids on tightly and store.

Jams

Home made jam – you can't beat it. It's not only a good way of storing surplus fruit for the winter, it's a great way of eating it too!

The preservation works by a combination of the boiling stage, which kills micro-organisms and de-activates enzymes, and the high sugar content of the product, which inhibits the growth of bacteria that may contaminate the jam later. Low sugar jam can be made, but it will be more runny, will need to be kept in the fridge and won't store so long.

There are whole books dedicated to jam-making, so I'm not going into too much detail here, but let's look at the basics:

1. Choose fruit that is just ripe or nearly ripe for jam-making.

2. Pectin and acid are both important in getting jam to set. Fruits high in both are apples, currants, gooseberries and plums. If your strawberry jam is just too runny then either combine the fruit with one rich in pectin and acid, or add commercial pectins and lemon juice.

3. Heat the washed fruit in a pan, adding a little water if necessary. Do not use iron pans, which will react with the acidic fruit and taint the flavour. Simmer for 15–45 minutes until broken down to a pulp.

4. Add the sugar: 60% by weight. Stir to dissolve and bring back to the boil.

5. Boil hard until setting point, which may be a few minutes or even up to 20. To test for setting point place a small blob of the mixture on a cold plate. After 1 minute it should have formed a skin which wrinkles when you touch it.

6. Remove from the heat immediately, skim off any scum from the surface, then stir and spoon the jam into jars which have been warmed in the oven.

7. Cover the surface with a waxed disc and then top the jar with either a cellulose cover held with an elastic band, or a plastic-coated metal lid screwed on tight while hot. Boil metal lids first to ensure they are sterile.

8. Cool, label, store, eat, enjoy!

Note that the addition of 60% by weight of sugar is critical for the best preservation, as any less than this will allow micro-organisms to start the jam fermenting. After opening it is a good idea to keep jars of jam in the fridge – especially if the proportion of sugar is suspect – to reduce growth of yeasts, bacteria or fungi.

Jellies are essentially jams made out of the fruit's juice. After cooking to a pulp strain the mixture and then continue with the juice, adding the sugar after returning to the boil.

A few recipes are suggested in Part Two, but again, experimentation with mixtures of fruits can yield satisfying results.

Fermenting

If you transform a fruit or vegetable into something different, can this be classed as storage? Tricky question. But the point is that when you are deciding what to do with your abundance of apples to see you through the winter for example, making cider is an important consideration!

As there are many detailed books on the home brewing of ciders, wines and beers this is not the place to compete with them. The making of cider is explored more in Part Two under Apples, but as so many fruits and vegetables can be made into wines we'll discuss some of the basics here.

The general idea is that yeasts (usually introduced, although natural ones do occur on the surface of most fruits) grow and multiply using sugar, and produce alcohol as a result. Cleanliness is vital at all stages to prevent fungi and other micro-organisms from spoiling the end product. All equipment and bottles must be sterilised either by boiling, or by washing with a chemical sterilising solution.

1. First the fruits or vegetables are washed then chopped, crushed, mashed or pressed.

2. Boiling water is added (sometimes simmering is needed) and this mixture can be left for a day.

3. The mixture is strained, sugar and yeast added and then it is poured into demijohns or other vessels which are then fitted with a fermentation lock (to exclude air, which will contain undesirable micro-organisms). If juice such as grape juice is being used it can go straight into the demijohn with the yeast, omitting stage 2.

4. The demijohns are left in a warm place to ferment – this could take a month or two.

5. 'Racking' is the procedure of siphoning the liquid into a clean vessel while leaving the sediment behind. This may be required a couple of times during the fermentation until the wine is clear.

6. When fermentation has ceased the liquid is then racked into sterile bottles, which are corked and stored somewhere cool and dark. Most wines improve after a few months, but some need a year!

Almost any fruit or vegetable can be made into wine. For specific techniques and recipes you should consult a wine-making book, although some suggestions are scattered throughout Part Two.

Part Two

The Produce

Apples

Windfalls and early maturing varieties do not store so well, so use these to make jam and chutney. Cooking apples are also best for jam making because of their high acid content. Late maturing varieties will be sweeter, so better for juice and making cider. Cox's and Bramley's keep particularly well.

Dry Storage For later-ripening fruit. Use only perfect specimens. Wrap in paper and place gently in crates or on shelves in a cool, frost-free, but not too dry place. Should keep until spring.

Jam Apples are often added to other fruits which may be lacking in acid for jam-making – for example see **Blackberry and Apple Jam** under **Blackberries.**

Freeze Either fresh after peeling and removing core, or after stewing for later use in pies, crumbles etc..

Chutney Apples are a useful addition to a variety of chutneys – see **Marrow and Apple Chutney** under **Marrows,** and **Green Tomato Chutney** under **Tomatoes,** as examples.

Juice Extract the juice using a fruit press or electric juicer. Freshly-pressed juice will keep only for a day or two in the fridge before fermenting, but don't forget to freeze some. This can be done in plastic bags inside small boxes (e.g. juice cartons); when frozen, the boxes can be removed and the blocks of juice packed together. Empty plastic milk cartons can also be used for freezing juice, but they must be thoroughly cleaned, and don't forget to leave 5 cm space for expansion as the juice freezes.

Cider

Best to use a mixture of apple varieties for cider. A good way to use up over-ripe and bruised apples that wouldn't store well by other means. As with wine-making it is important that all the equipment used is clean.

1. Wash the apples and chop them roughly. Then crush them by pounding with a heavy wooden post in a strong bucket, or use a purpose-built crusher.

2. Put the pulp in a fruit press and apply pressure to extract the juice.

3. Pour the juice into a demijohn (or suitable fermenting vessel) and add yeast.

4. Fit a fermentation lock (to exclude air, which will contain undesirable micro-organisms), and leave in a warm place to ferment – this could take a couple of weeks.

5. Rack the liquid (siphon into a clean vessel while leaving the sediment behind) once or twice during the fermentation until the cider is clear.

6. When fermentation has ceased rack the cider into sterile bottles and store somewhere cool and dark. You can start drinking it at Christmas (assuming you started fermentation in October) although it will continue to improve if you can bear to leave some of it any longer!

Artichokes

The tubers of Jerusalem artichokes are an interesting alternative to potatoes, and can be cooked in all the same ways – roasted, baked, fried, boiled and so on. They are completely different from globe artichokes which produce large green edible heads. These should be harvested before they flower.

Jerusalem artichokes can be left in the ground until they are needed. If you are expecting hard frosts then either cover the plants with a thick layer of straw, or heel them into dry ground near the house. Once harvested the tubers will keep fresh for a few weeks if kept in a plastic bag in the fridge.

Dry storage   Pack Jerusalem artichoke tubers in sand in boxes. In a cool, frost-free building they should keep for a few months.

Freeze   The tubers of Jerusalem artichokes can be cooked and mashed to a purée before freezing in plastic boxes or bags. This purée can be used later in soups.

To freeze globe artichokes, remove the outer leaves and stalks of small heads and blanch for 6 minutes before freezing in plastic bags. To cook from frozen, boil for about 10 minutes.

Wine: Artichoke Wine
An interesting wine can be made from Jerusalem artichokes. See Part One for general instructions. Scrub and slice 3 kg of tubers, boil with 1 kg sugar in 5 litres water. Cool, add the yeast, and ferment.

Asparagus

Asparagus spears will appear in May and should be cut when they have reached about 120 cm tall. Cut them 50 cm below the soil surface with a long knife.

The quality of asparagus declines rapidly after cutting. It will only keep for a few days in the fridge, but standing the spears upright in a mug of water will extend this a little. For longer storage, freezing is the best option.

Freeze   Immediately after cutting wash well then blanch for 2 minutes (or 4 minutes for thick stems). Pack in plastic containers and freeze. To cook from frozen, boil for about 4 minutes.

It's true. It is a small holding.

Aubergines

It is quite easy to grow aubergines (also known as egg plants) in a greenhouse or polytunnel, and they are becoming increasingly popular. Do not let the purple, shiny fruits grow too large, but cut when about 15cm long. These will stay useable for several weeks in the fridge or can be frozen straight away.

a ubergine

Freeze After peeling, cut the aubergine into thick slices or chunks and then blanch for 4 minutes. Open-freeze before packing into containers. Thaw before adding to dishes (such as moussaka and ratatouille) for cooking.

Beans – Broad

Freezing is the best option for storing broad beans, but some varieties freeze better than others – check the details on seed packets. Large tough beans do not become tender by freezing, so harvest when small and tender.

Freeze After washing the shelled beans, blanch for 1 or 2 minutes depending on size. Open-freeze then bag up. To cook from frozen, boil for about 6 minutes.

Wine: Broad Bean Wine
See Part One for general instructions. Boil 2 kg of shelled beans in 5 litres water. Do not split or mash the beans but strain off the liquid. Then add sugar and yeast to the cooled liquid, and ferment.

Beans – French

Pick the pods while young and tender and eat or freeze as soon as possible after harvesting. If the pods are young there will be no need to string them.

Freeze Wash, trim the ends off and string if necessary. Blanch for 2 minutes before packing in plastic bags. To cook from frozen, boil for about 5 minutes.

Dry Haricot beans: some varieties are more suited to this than others. Leave the pods on the plants until they have turned yellow, then cut the plant at ground level and hang indoors to dry completely. When the pods have become brittle, shell the beans and leave on trays for a few days. Then store in a cool dry place in air-tight containers.

Beans – Runner

Freezing is the best option for runner beans, but some varieties freeze better than others – check the details on seed packets.

Freeze Wash, trim the ends off and string the beans. Slice into short lengths and blanch for 2 minutes before packing in plastic bags. To cook from frozen, boil for about 5 minutes.

Dry These can be dried in the same way as haricot beans. Leave the pods on the plants until they have turned yellow, then cut the plant at ground level and hang indoors to dry completely. When the pods have become brittle, shell the beans and leave on trays for a few days. Then store in a cool dry place in air-tight containers.

Salt: Salted Beans

Although salting is rarely used these days, and is much more time-consuming than freezing, I mention it here as salted beans are still favoured by some. Use 1 kg kitchen salt for every 3 kg beans. Wash, string and slice the beans, Pack in glass jars with layers of salt and beans, press down and cover. After a few days the beans will have shrunk down as the water is drawn out; add more beans and salt to fill the jar again. A thick brine is formed in the jar which will preserve the beans for a year or more. When needed, wash the beans well, soak in warm water for an hour, rinse and simmer in unsalted water until tender.

Beetroot

Pull beetroots for storage before they get too large and woody – from July to October. Twist the foliage off (cutting causes bleeding of the beets). Pickled beetroots are loved by so many that this process is a good preparation for eating as well as a good storage method.

Freeze   Small beetroots should first be washed and boiled as they are for 1 or 2 hours in salted water. Then the skins can be rubbed off (if desired), before slicing and packing in containers.

Pickle   Boil and skin as above before covering with vinegar in suitable jars. Either slice or, if small, pickle whole. Pickled beetroot can be used after a week and will be at their best for 3 months.

Dry storage   Gently remove the soil from undamaged beets and pack in sand in boxes. In a cool, frost-free building they should keep until spring.

Wine: Beetroot Wine

See Part One for general instructions. Boil 2 kg of diced, unpeeled beetroot in 3 litres water for 30 minutes, strain, stir in 1.75 kg sugar, and add the juice of a lemon. Then add yeast to the cooled liquid, and ferment. If you like ginger you may like to try adding some crushed ginger root with the lemon juice.

Blackberries

Pick blackberries when sun-ripened for the best flavour. They are low in acid so are often mixed with other fruit when making jam.

Freeze Fresh after removing stalks (open-freeze then bag up). Can also be frozen as a purée after stewing and sieving.

Jam: Blackberry and Apple Jam
2 kg blackberries, 1 kg cooking apples, 400 ml water, 3 kg sugar
Simmer the apples and blackberries until soft in separate pans with half the water each. Then mix together with the sugar, stir, boil, and keep boiling hard to setting point.

Bottle See Part One for methods. If heating in water, heat to simmering (88°C) in 30 minutes and hold this for a further 2 minutes. If heating in the oven, keep at 150°C for 40 minutes (for up to 2 kg fruit) or for 60 minutes (for up to 5 kg fruit).

Chutney: Blackberry Chutney
3 kg blackberries, 1 kg apples, 1 kg onions, 25 g salt, 1 kg sugar, 1 litre vinegar, spices of your choice (e.g. ginger, pepper, mustard)
Finely chop the apples and onions and add to the blackberries in a large pan. Add the vinegar, salt and spices and simmer for 1 hour. Sieve the chutney to remove the pips, then add the sugar, stir and simmer until it reaches a pulpy consistency. Jar up and seal.

Wine: Blackberry Wine
See Part One for general instructions. Dissolve 2 kg sugar in 5 litres of boiling water. When cool, add this liquid to 2 kg mashed blackberries. Then add the yeast, juice of 2 lemons and ferment.

Black Currants
(and Red and White Currants)

Pick when ripe and juicy! They may be fiddly to harvest and fiddly to prepare (after removing the stalks and calyx (top brown bit) from each currant you will have purple hands for sure) but it is well worth it. Black currant jam is a favourite and the freshly pressed juice tastes unbelievable, and is very good for you!

Freeze Fresh after removing stalks (open-freeze then bag up). Can also be frozen as a purée after stewing and sieving.

Jam: Black Currant Jam
2 kg black currants, 2 litres water, 3 kg sugar
Wash the currants, heat with the water and simmer until tender. Keep simmering and stirring until the pulp is thick then add the sugar. Stir, boil, and keep boiling hard until setting point.

Bottle See Part One for methods. If heating in water, heat to simmering (88°C) in 30 minutes and hold this for a further 2 minutes. If heating in the oven, keep at 150°C for 40 minutes (for up to 2 kg fruit) or for 60 minutes (for up to 5 kg fruit).

Juice Extract the juice using a fruit press or electric juicer. Freshly-pressed juice will keep only for a day or two in the fridge before fermenting – but don't forget to freeze some. This can be done in plastic bags inside small boxes (e.g. juice cartons); when frozen the boxes can be removed and the blocks of juice packed together. Empty plastic milk cartons can also be used for freezing juice, but they must be thoroughly cleaned, and don't forget to leave 5 cm space for expansion as the juice freezes. You may wish to dilute the juice for drinking, or try mixing with other juices – black currant and apple juice for example.

Wine: Black Currant Wine

See Part One for general instructions. Crush 1 kg of black currants and add 1 kg chopped sultanas, 2.5 kg sugar and the juice of a lemon. Stir in 3 litres of boiling water. Then add yeast to the cooled liquid, and ferment.

Sorry, we're out of lettuce. May I recommend the new potatoes?

Broccoli
(and Calabrese)

The big green heads you buy in the supermarket, which are called 'broccoli', are actually calabrese. Real broccoli varieties are generally the sort you can continually cut heads (or spears) from through the season, such as purple sprouting. By careful choice of different varieties – early-sprouting, late-sprouting and calabrese for example – you can have fresh broccoli available for much of the year.

Otherwise, all types of broccoli and calabrese are best stored by freezing. Harvest them before the tiny flowers open.

Freeze Blanch for 1 to 3 minutes first depending on stem thickness (so sort them into batches of the same thickness first!). Broccoli heads can often lock together as they freeze, resulting in one green block that you have to smash apart, so it is a good candidate for open-freezing first. To cook from frozen, boil for about 5 minutes.

Brussels Sprouts

Keep cutting Brussels sprouts while they are small, working up the stem of the plant, and you will be harvesting these from October to February. Freeze plenty for use throughout the rest of the year.

Harvest only a few from each plant at a time. When all the sprouts are gone you can use the top of the plant like a cabbage.

Freeze   Pick while they are small and remove the outer leaves. Blanch for 2 minutes before cooling and bagging-up. To cook from frozen, boil for about 7 minutes.

Cabbages

Winter cabbages are best for dry storage; red cabbages pickle well. This is another vegetable where use of a selection of varieties, which mature at different times of the year, will enable you to harvest fresh cabbages all year round.

Dry Storage   Cut winter cabbages at the end of autumn, remove the outer leaves, and store nestled in straw or shredded paper in crates. They should be placed in a cool, dry building where the cabbages will stay in good condition until spring.

Pickle   Shred the cabbage, layer with salt and leave for 24 hours. Rinse the salt off, pack into jars, and cover with vinegar. Pickled cabbage can be used after a week and should be consumed within 3 months or it loses its crunch!

Freeze   Wash and shred before blanching for 1 minute and freezing in plastic bags. To cook from frozen, boil for about 5 minutes.

Carrots

If you are short of space in your freezer just freeze the young tender carrots, putting the larger ones into dry storage.

Freeze Trim, wash and blanch for 4 minutes before freezing in plastic bags. Small ones can be frozen whole, large ones can be sliced or diced. Peeling first will depend on your taste, and whether they are organic or not! Although the skins of many vegetables are good for you, it is also thought that harmful chemicals such as pesticides accumulate in the skins. To cook from frozen, boil for about 10 minutes, or add frozen to casseroles.

Dry storage Leave until October then pull up and gently remove the soil from undamaged carrots. Trim off the foliage and pack in sand in boxes; in a cool, frost-free building they should keep until spring.

Clamp Rarely used these days, but can be a useful temporary technique for larger quantities. See 'Clamping' in Part One for details.

Wine: Carrot Wine
See Part One for general instructions. Scrub and grate 5 kg of carrots, boil with 2 kg sugar in 5 litres water. Cool, add the yeast, and ferment.

Cauliflower

Cut heads of cauliflower can be hung in a cool building for several weeks before use. Freeze for longer storage, and don't forget to make some fabulous Piccalilli. There are summer, autumn and winter varieties of cauliflower available that mature at different times of the year.

Freeze Cut into florets and blanch for 2 minutes before freezing. Adding a little lemon juice to the blanching water will help the cauliflower keep its white colour. To cook from frozen, boil the florets for about 6 minutes.

Pickle Cauliflower is often the principle vegetable in **Piccalilli:**
2 kg of mixed vegetables (cauliflower, marrow, small onions, gherkins for example) 10 g turmeric, 20 g ground ginger, 20 g mustard, 20 g cornflour, 200 g sugar, 1.5 litres vinegar
Break the cauliflower into tiny florets, and cube the marrow and gherkins. Peel the onions. Soak all the vegetables in brine for 24 hours. Put the sugar and spices in a pan and stir in the vinegar. Add the vegetables, stir and heat to boiling. Simmer until the vegetables are tender but not pulped. Add the cornflour (mixed in a little vinegar), stir and boil a further 3 minutes before jarring up and sealing.

Celeriac

You can eat the leaves and roots of celeriac. Both taste like celery – in fact it is also known as turnip-rooted celery. Unlike many other vegetables the texture and flavour are just as good in large, older roots, so grow them as big as you like! Harvesting will start in October, but like some other roots they can be left in the ground until spring. If hard frosts are expected just cover the crowns with a thick layer of straw. The following storage techniques refer to the root.

Freeze   Wash, peel, cut the root into chunks and blanch for 4 minutes before open-freezing. These chunks are a great addition to soups and stews. They can also be frozen as a purée.

Dry storage   Leave until October or November then pull up and remove the soil from the roots. Trim off the foliage and pack in sand in boxes; in a cool, frost-free building they should keep until spring.

Wine: Celeriac Wine

See Part One for general instructions. Scrub and grate 3 kg of celeriac roots, boil with 2 kg sugar in 5 litres water. Cool, add the yeast, and ferment.

Celery

Celery can be left in the ground until it is needed. Frost protection is rarely required – in fact there are some who say that the flavour improves after the first frost.

Harvested sticks will keep fresh in the fridge for some days, especially if stood upright in a mug of water.

Freeze Wash well then cut into small chunks or slices. Blanch for 2 or 3 minutes, depending on chunk size, then cool and bag up before placing in the freezer. Add frozen to stews.

Cherries

Cherries are not very acidic, so not so good for jam making. Pick when they are ripe and of good colour, but not too soft. Use the best for freezing and bottling.

Freeze   Fresh after removing stones. Open-freeze then pack in plastic bags or containers.

Bottle   See Part One for methods. Cherries can be bottled with or without the stones. If heating in water, heat to simmering (88°C) in 30 minutes and hold this for a further 10 minutes. If heating in the oven, keep at 150°C for 50 minutes (for up to 2 kg fruit) or for 70 minutes (for up to 5 kg fruit).

Jam: Cherry Jam

4 kg stoned cherries, 3 kg sugar, 4 lemons

Wash and stone the cherries. Heat with the juice of the lemons and simmer until tender. Add the sugar, stir, boil, and keep boiling hard until setting point.

Chicory

There are two main types of chicory. Those that are forced (kept in the dark) produce heads (known as 'chicons') – these are grown from the cut roots of the plant in late autumn and should be harvested in the winter when about 15 cm tall. Exposure to light will cause them to become bitter so they should be frozen straight away, or kept in the dark and used as soon as possible. Non-forced varieties produce heads more like lettuce, which can be left in situ throughout autumn until needed. In plastic bags in the fridge they will stay fresh for about 4 weeks.

Freeze Trim the heads of forced chicory and blanch for 3 minutes before freezing in plastic bags. Adding a good squeeze of lemon juice to the blanching water will help the chicons keep their white colour. To cook from frozen, boil for about 10 minutes.

Cucumbers

Wrapped in cling-film cucumber will stay fresh in the fridge for a week or two. Freezing is not an option as the texture disintegrates. Keep harvesting the fruits before they grow too large – more will come!

Pickle Small cucumbers or gherkins pickle well. Gherkins are just a variety of cucumber that produces small, warty fruits that are ideal for pickling. First, wash with a scouring pad (which will also remove the tiny prickles) and dry. Then cover with salt, or a brine solution, for a day before packing in jars and topping up with vinegar. Don't forget the flavour improves after a few months!

Endive

Like lettuce, endive does not store well, but it can be kept in the ground and harvested throughout the winter this is not a problem. Successional sowing throughout the summer will provide harvestable endive heads until the next spring.

It is a good idea to blanch the heads before harvesting to reduce the bitterness. This is NOT the same blanching you do before freezing, so turn the kettle off! In this case to blanch means 'to turn white' and you do this by covering the head of the plant with a pot to keep it in the dark. Begin this about 3 months after sowing, and harvest about a month later.

Cut heads will stay fresh in plastic bags in the fridge for up to a week, but must be kept dark or they will become bitter.

Fennel

The feathery leaves of common fennel can be used for flavouring. They have a strong aniseed taste – see Herbs for storage techniques. As the leaves are very fine they are more suited to freezing than to drying.

Florence fennel also has feathery leaves which taste of aniseed and can be treated in the same way. But, in addition, Florence fennel produces edible bulbs (swollen stem bases), also tasting of aniseed, which should be harvested when the size of a tennis ball in late summer.

Freeze Trim and cut into slices before blanching for 3 minutes. Pack into plastic bags and place in the freezer. To cook from frozen, boil for about 8 minutes or add frozen to stews.

Garlic

Garlic is surprisingly easy to grow. It takes little space and little effort to produce enough strongly-flavoured bulbs to last you all year.

After the tops have died down in mid-summer, the garlic bulbs should be carefully lifted on a sunny day and left on the ground to dry. The excess soil can then be gently brushed off and the bulbs stored in a cool, dry, frost-free place (not in the kitchen, or they will soon start to sprout!)

They can be strung and hung like onions or simply left in boxes. If the conditions are right they will stay in good condition for nearly a year, although some will start to sprout as the weather warms up again next spring. Either use these straight away or plant them for your next crop!

Gooseberries

Gooseberries that are young and hard have a higher acid and pectin content so are better for jam making. Use later, softer ones for chutneys or wine.

Freeze Top and tail before freezing fresh in plastic bags.. Can also be frozen as a purée after stewing and sieving.

Jam: Gooseberry Jam

2.5 kg gooseberries, 1 litre water, 3 kg sugar
Wash and top and tail the gooseberries. Heat with the water and simmer until tender. Keep simmering and stirring until the pulp is thick then add the sugar. Stir, boil, and keep boiling hard until setting point.

Bottle See Part One for methods. Top and tail the gooseberries first. If heating in water, heat to simmering (88°C) in 30 minutes and hold this for a further 2 minutes. If heating in the oven, keep at 150°C for 40 minutes (for up to 2 kg fruit) or for 60 minutes (for up to 5 kg fruit).

Chutney: Gooseberry Chutney

2 kg gooseberries, 400 g onions, 20 g salt, 500 g sugar, 400 ml water, 600 ml vinegar, spices of your choice (e.g. ginger, pepper, chillies)
Finely chop the gooseberries and onions and simmer in the water until very soft. Add the vinegar, sugar, salt and spices, stir and simmer until a pulpy consistency is achieved. Jar up and seal.

Wine: Gooseberry Wine

See Part One for general instructions. Add 5 litres of boiling water to 3 kg gooseberries and 2 kg sugar. After 24 hours add the yeast and ferment.

another goosegog   a goosegog

Grapes

Plenty of grape varieties are available, both white and black, for growing in cooler climates. Harvest the bunches by cutting them off with scissors when the grapes are ripe.

To keep cut bunches of grapes fresh, cut them with a piece of branch attached, stick this in a jar of water and store in a cool dark cupboard for up to two months.

Freeze   Fresh after removing stalks (and pips if desired!).

Juice   Extract the juice using a fruit press. Freshly pressed juice will keep only for a day or two in the fridge before fermenting – don't forget to freeze some. This can be done in plastic bags inside small boxes (e.g. juice cartons); when frozen, the boxes can be removed and the blocks of juice packed together. Empty plastic milk cartons can also be used for freezing juice, but they must be thoroughly cleaned, and don't forget to leave 5cm space for expansion as the juice freezes.

Wine   See Part One for general instructions. Ferment with the grape skins in for red wine, sieve the skins out and you get white wine, whether the grapes are red, black or green! For every 10 litres of juice add 500 g sugar and the yeast before fermenting.

Herbs

Pick herbs for storing on the morning of a dry day shortly before they flower. Choose the growing tips for the best flavour.

Freeze Best way of keeping the flavour. The most useful method is to chop the herbs and freeze small amounts in ice-cube trays in water or vegetable cooking-oil. In each cube put about as much as you like to use in your favourite recipes. Either freeze each herb separately or make up your own mixtures. Once frozen, the cubes can be tipped into plastic bags and placed back in the freezer so you don't run out of cube trays. Label carefully as ice cubes containing green bits look remarkably similar! When needed, simply add a herby ice cube or two to your cooking. If frying, make it a herby oil cube!

Large sprigs of herbs such as parsley, coriander and mint can simply be washed and frozen in plastic bags. They can then be crushed, straight from frozen, when required.

Dry A warm, dry place is needed for drying. An airing cupboard may do but will take a few days, whereas a warm oven (45°–55°C) will take a few hours. Herbs can be hung in bunches or laid out on a baking sheet. When the leaves are dry, crumble them into glass jars, seal, label and store in a cool, dark place.

If you are collecting the seed rather than the foliage – coriander for example – simply hang the whole plant to dry in a warm sunny room. Then shake the seeds off in a bag, and store in glass jars in a cool, dark place.

Pickle Many herbs can be added to vinegars to impart their flavour. Mint sauce can be simply made by finely chopping mint leaves in a little vinegar (add some sugar just before using). Other flavoured vinegars can be used in salad dressings and to pickle other vegetables.

To make a **herb vinegar** for salad dressings, crush a few leaves of the herb (or herbs) and add to a jar of wine vinegar or cider vinegar. Keep in a warm place for a few weeks, shaking the jar every now and again. Then strain out the leaves and use, or bottle, the vinegar. Try it with thyme, rosemary, tarragon, basil, bay, dill or your other favourite herbs.

The same technique can be used with oils like olive oil and sunflower oil to give them a herb flavour. Great for cooking with as well as for salad dressings!

Kale

Kale is one of the hardiest of vegetables – it can survive the sharpest of frosts – so you can be harvesting the crop from December through to March or April with no need for protection. It's very good for you too – the dark green colour is a clue that the leaves are full of iron and vitamin C. Old leaves can be bitter, so regularly harvest the young tender shoots. Once the plant has gone through the first frosts this will reduce the bitterness too. Freezing the tender shoots ensures you have a year-round supply at your finger tips.

Freeze Blanch the young shoots for 1 minute before chopping and bagging-up for freezing. You can open-freeze little piles of leaves or simply bag up portion sizes. To cook from frozen, boil for about 5 minutes.

Kohlrabi

Kohlrabi grows fast and produces edible globes or swollen stem bases which should be harvested at about tennis ball size within just a couple of months from sowing. They can be left in the ground until early winter but don't let the nutty-tasting globes grow too big. When lifted they will store for a few weeks in the fridge, or should be frozen straight away.

Freeze   Trim, peel and chop into chunks before blanching for 2 minutes. Open-freeze before bagging-up. To cook from frozen, boil for about 10 minutes or add some frozen chunks directly to stews. Alternatively the globes can be peeled, chopped and boiled for 20 minutes before mashing and freezing in a cooked state.

Leeks

Leeks are extremely hardy and you should be harvesting them for at least six months of the year: November to April. They can be left in the ground until they are needed, otherwise freezing is really the only suitable storage method. They can be harvested at any size, the smaller ones having the greater flavour.

Freeze Top and tail and wash carefully to make sure there is no soil left between the layers of skin. Slice thickly and blanch for 3 minutes before bagging-up and freezing. To cook from frozen, boil for 8 minutes, or add the frozen slices to stews.

Lettuces

Lettuce does not store well! It will keep for up to a week in a plastic bag in the fridge, but it's better to leave it in the ground until the day it is needed. If possible, cut the heads in the morning for the crispest leaves.

Otherwise, the key is successional sowing, and to use different varieties that become ready at different times of the year. Lettuces cannot be frozen (the leaves disintegrate to a mush), and mid-winter varieties will have to be grown under heated glass. If you can do this, and also plant spring, summer and early winter crops, then you can have fresh lettuce from the garden 12 months of the year.

Marrows
(Courgettes, Squashes, Pumpkins)

Marrows, pumpkins and squashes should be left on the plants until the first frost is expected. Then cut and store in a cool dry building, either hung in nets or placed on shelves. They will stay in good condition until mid-winter.

Marrows can be made into wine and jam and are a great addition to chutneys.

Freeze   Courgettes can be frozen after washing, slicing thickly, and blanching for 1 minute. To cook from frozen, boil for about 2 minutes or add frozen to stir-fries.

Jam: Damson and Marrow Jam
2 kg damsons, 2 kg marrow cubes, 750 ml water, 4 kg sugar
Heat the damsons with half the water and simmer until tender. Sieve to remove the stones. Simmer the marrow cubes with the rest of the water until pulped. Mix the pulps, bring back to a simmer, then add the sugar. Stir, boil, and keep boiling hard until setting point.

Chutney
Flesh from marrows, courgettes, pumpkins and squashes can be used to add bulk and texture to all sorts of chutneys.

Marrow and Apple Chutney
2 kg marrow, 1 kg apples, 500 g onions, 75 g salt, 500 g sugar, 2 litres vinegar, spices of your choice (e.g. ginger, pepper, chillies)
Peel the marrow and cut the flesh into small cubes. Cover with salt overnight then rinse. Put the marrow in a large pan with the finely-chopped onions and apples and the spices. Heat gently and simmer until tender. Add the vinegar and sugar, stir and simmer until it reaches a pulpy consistency. Jar up and seal.

Wine: Marrow Wine
See Part One for general instructions. Add 5litres of boiling water to 3 kg chopped, ripe marrow and 2 kg sugar. After 24 hours add the yeast and ferment.

Mushrooms

If drying or freezing mushrooms, this must be done as soon as possible after picking. Pick by twisting rather than cutting the stems. Ideally mushrooms should not be washed or peeled: any dirt should just be wiped off the caps. If you need to keep them fresh in the fridge then a paper bag should be used, as plastic bags just make them sweat and disintegrate faster.

Dry Slice, then dry in a warm oven (45°–55°C) for a few hours. Store in an air-tight jar in a cool, dark place; they are then a great addition to soups and stews.

Freeze Button mushrooms can be frozen whole, or large ones can be sliced. If frozen raw they will keep well only for about a month; if first cooked by frying for a few minutes they will keep better – up to 3 months.
Add frozen mushrooms to soups, stews, casseroles etc..

Pickle Put clean mushrooms in a pan and cover with vinegar. Season with salt, pepper and spice if desired. Heat gently until the mushrooms have visibly shrunk, then jar up, covering with the hot vinegar.

Okra

Okra can be grown quite successfully in a greenhouse or polytunnel. The plants produce edible pods called 'ladies' fingers' which can be used in curries, stews and stir-fries. Keep cutting the pods while young: 5-8 cm long and bright green.

Freeze   Trim off the stalks and blanch the pods whole for 2 minutes before cooling and freezing in plastic bags. To cook from frozen, boil for 5 minutes or add frozen to stews or curries. The pods can be sliced while still frozen.

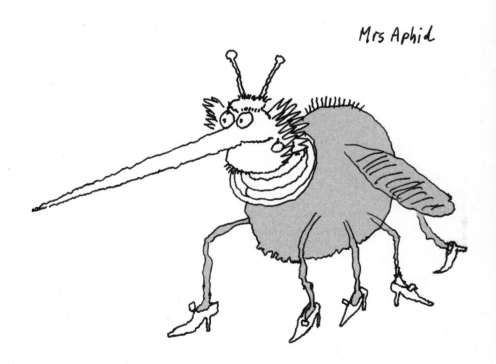

Mrs Aphid

Onions

The most essential vegetable, and easy to store! After the tops have fully died down at the end of summer, onions should be lifted on a sunny day and left on the ground. They then need a few weeks to dry. The easiest method is to lay them in trays (clean seed trays will do) which are left in the sun, but brought indoors if rain threatens.

Hang   When dry, the best specimens can be hung in nets or strung together. They will store well in a cool dry place until the end of spring. To start your string take four onions and tie the stalks together, then tie the knotted stalks to a piece of string. Hang this from the roof of your store and then add further onions, one at a time, by tying their stalks around the string and sliding them down to meet the others. Don't add so many that the string breaks!

Freeze   Skin, slice and blanch for 2 minutes before freezing. Small onions can be frozen whole. When needed, add frozen to soups, stews etc..

Pickle   Peel small and medium-sized onions and soak in brine for a day before drying (on kitchen paper) and covering in vinegar in suitable jars. Don't forget to leave them to mature before eating – see if you can wait until Christmas!

Chutney   Onions are of course a vital ingredient in most chutneys – see the various chutney recipes throughout Part Two.

Parsnips

Parsnips can be left in the ground until they are needed. If there are still some left in the ground at the end of winter they can be lifted then for storage.

Freeze   Trim, peel, and cut into chunks before blanching for 3 minutes. Place in plastic bags in the freezer. To cook from frozen, boil for about 10 minutes or add frozen chunks direct to soups or stews. Fresh parsnips can also be boiled and mashed and frozen in the cooked state. Try mixing roots in mashes – carrot and parsnip for example.

Dry storage   Pull parsnips up, and gently remove the soil from undamaged roots. Trim off the foliage, pack the roots in sand in boxes, and store in a cool, frost-free building.

Clamp   Rarely used these days, but can be a useful temporary technique for larger quantities. See 'Clamping' in Part One for details.

Wine: Parsnip Wine

Parsnip wine has been a favourite for many years – see Part One for general instructions. For each 2 kg of parsnips you will need to add 5 litres of water. After boiling and pressing add 1.5 kg sugar and the yeast. Then ferment.

the humble parsnip

Peas

Peas are well known for deteriorating rapidly after picking, or at least for losing their sweetness. The sugar is converted to starch within minutes of harvesting! So only pick the pods when you are going to use or freeze them straight away. When picking, hold the plant stem with one hand while you pull the pods off with the other, as otherwise you may break the stem.

Freeze   Pick while tender, shell and blanch for 1 minute before bagging-up and freezing. To cook from frozen, boil for about 5 minutes. Varieties where you eat the pod too, such as mangetout and sugar snap, can be frozen whole or sliced, after blanching for two minutes.

Dry   Leave the pods on the plants until they have turned yellow, then cut the plant at ground level and hang indoors to dry completely. When the pods have become brittle, shell the peas and leave on trays for a few days. Then store in a cool dry place in air-tight containers.

Wine: Pea Pod Wine
See Part One for general instructions. Boil 3 kg chopped pea pods with 5 litres of water and 1 kg sugar. When cool, add the yeast and ferment.

Peaches
(and Apricots and Nectarines)

Time your picking of these fruit carefully: ripe but not too soft. Use the best for eating now, bottling and freezing, second best for jam, and worst for chutney!

Freeze   Either fresh after peeling and removing stones, or after stewing.

Bottle See Part One for methods. These fruits can be bottled with or without the stones as desired. If heating in water, heat to simmering (88°C) in 30 minutes and hold this for a further 10 minutes. If heating in the oven, keep at 150°C for 50 minutes (for up to 2 kg fruit) or for 70 minutes (for up to 5 kg fruit).

Jam: Apricot Jam
2.5 kg apricots, 2.5 kg sugar, 500 ml water
Wash and halve the apricots and remove the stones. (Note that as most of the pectin is in the stones, it helps to cook a few stones in the mixture and remove these as you jar up). Heat the apricots with the water and simmer until tender. Add the sugar, stir, boil, and keep boiling hard to setting point.

Pears

Pears do not store well! They don't make jam well either and go brown if frozen. The best bet is bottling and dry storage, although they won't keep as long as apples.

Dry Storage Use only perfect specimens, wrap in paper and place gently in crates or on shelves in a cool, frost-free, but not too dry place.

Bottle See Part One for methods. Peel, halve and core the pears first. Keep under water with lemon juice added to prevent them turning brown before bottling. If heating in water, heat to simmering (88°C) in 30 minutes and hold this for a further 40 minutes. If heating in the oven, keep at 150°C for 70 minutes (for up to 2 kg fruit) or for 90 minutes (for up to 5 kg fruit).

Juice Extract the juice using a fruit press or electric juicer. Freshly-pressed juice will keep only for a day or two in the fridge before fermenting, but don't forget to freeze some. This can be done in plastic bags inside small boxes (e.g. juice cartons). When frozen, the boxes can be removed and the blocks of juice packed together. Empty plastic milk cartons can also be used for freezing juice, but they must be thoroughly cleaned – and don't forget to leave 5cm space for expansion as the juice freezes.

Wine: Pear Wine

See Part One for general instructions. Dissolve 2 kg sugar in 5 litres of boiling water. Cool the liquid and add 5 kg minced pears and the juice of a lemon. Add the yeast and ferment.

Perry   This is the pear equivalent of cider and made in exactly the same way – see **Cider** under **Apples** for instructions. To make the best perry, however, you need to grow perry pear varieties, such as Green Horse, Malvern Hills and Merrylegs!

Ah, I believe we have a table in the corner

Peppers
(Capsicum and Chilli)

Best grown in the greenhouse or polytunnel. Most capsicums grow green fruits which gradually turn red if left on the plant in the sun – they can be harvested as desired (some prefer the taste of green, some the taste of red, and some can't tell the difference!). Both capsicums and chilli peppers will stay fresh for several weeks in the fridge.

Freeze Both capsicums and chilli peppers can be frozen for later use in casseroles, curries etc.. First remove the stalks, then cut in half and scrape out the seeds and white pith. Blanch capsicums for 3 minutes, smaller chillies for 1 minute. Bag up when cool, and freeze.

red pepper

green pepper

Plums
(and Damsons and Greengages)

Most plums make good jam, purple plums are best for freezing and chutneys. Pick when ripe but still hard.

Freeze – fresh after removing stones, or after stewing. You may also like to skin them first, or they can be easily skinned after freezing by immersing the frozen plums in hot water for a minute or two, after which the skins will slide off when the fruit is squeezed.

Bottle See Part One for methods. These fruits can be bottled with or without stones as desired. If heating in water, heat to simmering (88°C) in 30 minutes and hold this for a further 10 minutes. If heating in the oven, keep at 150°C for 50 minutes (for up to 2 kg fruit) or for 70 minutes (for up to 5 kg fruit).

Jam: Plum Jam

3 kg plums, 1 litre water, 3 kg sugar

Wash the plums, cut them in half and remove the stones. (Note that as most of the pectin is in the stones, it helps to cook a few stones in the mixture and remove these as you jar up). Heat with the water and simmer until tender. Keep simmering and stirring until the pulp is thick then add the sugar. Stir, boil, and keep boiling hard until setting point.

See also **Damson and Marrow Jam** under **Marrows**

Wine: Greengage Wine

See Part One for general instructions. Remove the stones from 3 kg of greengages and add 2 kg sugar and 5 litres boiling water. Cool, add the yeast, and ferment.

Chutney: Plum Chutney

1 kg stoned plums, 500 g apples, 500 g onions, 500 g raisins, 25 g salt, 200 g sugar, 600 ml vinegar, spices of your choice (e.g. ginger, allspice, nutmeg, cloves)

Finely chop the apples and onions and add to the plums in a large pan. Add the other ingredients, stir and simmer until a pulpy consistency is achieved. Jar up and seal.

It's not just a pot.
It's a much treasured small-holding.

Potatoes

Like onions, potatoes are an essential crop – easy to grow and easy to store. Once the foliage has died down at the end of summer, cut the stems off at ground level (and remove) but leave the tubers in the ground for a further week or two. Then carefully dig up the potatoes on a dry day and leave on the surface to dry for a few hours. Throw away any green potatoes (which are a result of exposure to the sun whilst growing) as these are poisonous.

Dry storage   Once dry, the tubers can be stored in boxes or paper sacks in the dark in a dry building. They should keep in good condition until spring, but check regularly and remove any that are rotting.

Clamp   Potatoes are the classic roots for clamping. The process is used these days only for larger quantities. See 'Clamping' in Part One for details.

Freeze   Smaller, new potatoes can be frozen after blanching for 3 minutes. Or peel and slice into chips, blanch in oil, drain, and freeze in bags. Thaw chips before deep-frying. Can also be frozen after cooking: roast or mashed.

Potato clamp

Radishes

If you want to eat radishes all year round you can achieve this with a selection of varieties that mature at different times of the year. They are easy to grow but don't restrict yourself to salad use – winter radishes can be cooked or pickled.

Dry storage Trim off the foliage and pack in sand in boxes. In a cool, frost-free building they should keep for several months.

Pickle Winter radishes can grow large, so best to scrub the skins clean and slice before layering with salt (or putting in brine) and leaving for 24 hours. Rinse the salt off, pack into jars, and cover with vinegar.

Raspberries
(and Loganberries)

Excellent for freezing, and for jam making and bottling. Pick when large and well-coloured, before they go soft.

Freeze Fresh after removing stalks (open-freeze then bag up). Can also be frozen as a purée after stewing and sieving.

Bottle See Part One for methods. If heating in water, heat to simmering (88°C) in 30 minutes and hold this for a further 2 minutes. If heating in the oven, keep at 150°C for 40 minutes (for up to 2 kg fruit) or for 60 minutes (for up to 5 kg fruit).

Jam: Raspberry Jam

2 kg raspberries, 2k g sugar

Heat the raspberries and gently simmer until tender. Then add the sugar, stir, boil, and keep boiling hard until setting point.

See also **Rhubarb and Loganberry Jam** under **Rhubarb**

Wine: Loganberry Wine

See Part One for general instructions.Mash 3 kg of loganberries with 1 kg sultanas. Add 3 litres of boiling water and stir well. Strain (ensure all the pips are removed), then add 2.5 kg of sugar. Cool, add the yeast, and ferment.

Rhubarb

Rhubarb makes good jam, wine and chutneys. Use the young, spring shoots for freezing and bottling.

Freeze   Simply cut into chunks and open-freeze before bagging-up. Blanching for 1 minute will retain the colour, but it is not necessary.

Bottle   See Part One for methods. Cut the rhubarb into short chunks. If heating in water, heat to simmering (88°C) in 30 minutes and hold this for a further 2 minutes. If heating in the oven, keep at 150°C for 40 minutes (for up to 2 kg fruit) or for 60 minutes (for up to 5 kg fruit).

Jam: Rhubarb and Loganberry Jam

2 kg rhubarb, 1 kg loganberries or raspberries, 400 ml water, 3 kg sugar
Cut the rhubarb into chunks, heat in the water and simmer until tender. Add the berries then simmer further until they are tender. Then add the sugar, stir, boil, and keep boiling hard until setting point.

Wine: Rhubarb Wine

See Part One for general instructions. For each 10 kg of rhubarb you will need to add 7 litres of water. After soaking and pressing add 1.5 kg sugar and the yeast. Then ferment.

Chutney: Rhubarb Chutney

2 kg rhubarb, 500 g onions, 20 g salt, 1 kg sugar, 1 litre vinegar, spices of your choice (e.g. ginger, mixed spice)
Slice the rhubarb into short pieces and place with the finely-chopped onions, salt, sugar and spices in a pan. Add half the vinegar and simmer the mixture until tender. Then add the rest of the vinegar, stir and simmer until a pulpy consistency is achieved. Jar up and seal.

Salsify
(and Scorzonera)

These roots are hardy and can be left in the ground until required. Expect to harvest them from the end of October through to April. They can be treated like parsnips and are both delicious! It is worth lifting a few in early winter and putting into storage for use when the ground is too frozen to dig.

Freeze   Peel, trim and cut into chunks before blanching for 4 minutes. Then bag up and freeze. To cook from frozen, boil for about 10 minutes or add frozen chunks direct to soups or stews.

Dry storage   Lift in November, trim off the foliage and pack in sand in boxes. In a cool, frost-free building they should keep for several months.

Spinach

By choosing the correct varieties you can have spinach ready for picking in the garden all year round. Pick a few leaves from each plant, and use or freeze as soon as possible after harvesting. Wash the leaves very well in several changes of water to get rid of any soil. There's nothing worse than spinach that makes your teeth squeak!

Freeze Wash the leaves well then blanch for 2 minutes. Cool and squeeze out excess water before freezing in plastic bags. It will freeze as a solid lump so fill each bag with only as much spinach as you will need for one meal. To cook from frozen, boil for about 5 minutes.

Strawberries

Freeze the smaller strawberries and make jam with the rest. Bottle if you don't have a freezer or if you prefer this method.

Freeze   Open-freeze before packing into plastic bags or containers. Can also be frozen as a purée after processing.

Jam: Strawberry Jam
2 kg strawberries, 1 lemon, 1.75 kg sugar
Heat the strawberries with the juice of the lemon, stir and gently simmer until tender. Then add the sugar, stir, boil, and keep boiling hard until setting point.

Bottle   See Part One for methods. Halve and wash the strawberries first. If heating in water, heat to simmering (88°C) in 30 minutes and hold this for a further 2 minutes. If heating in the oven, keep at 150°C for 40 minutes (for up to 2 kg fruit) or for 60 minutes (for up to 5 kg fruit).

Wine: Strawberry Wine
See Part One for general instructions.Wash 2 kg of sound strawberries and add to 2 kg sugar and 4 litres of boiling water. Stir and mash the fruit well. Cool, add the yeast, and ferment.

Swedes

Swedes can be dug up as soon as they are large enough to use. They are very hardy and can be left in the soil until required. Expect to be harvesting from September to March.

Freeze   Wash, trim and cut into chunks before blanching for 3 minutes. Cool and freeze in plastic bags. To cook from frozen, boil for about 8 minutes.

Dry storage   Pull up and gently remove the soil from undamaged roots. Twist off the foliage and pack the roots in sand in boxes. Store in a cool, frost-free building.

Clamp   If you have a lot of swedes, you can store them in a clamp where they will keep better than turnips.

Sweet Corn

Like peas, sweet corn loses its sweetness rapidly from the moment the cobs are picked. The sugar is converted to starch within minutes of harvesting. So pick the cobs only when you are going to eat or freeze them straight away.

Freeze Pull off the outer leaves and silks, trim the stalk, and blanch for 5 minutes. After cooling wrap each cob in foil or cling-film before placing in the freezer. Thaw before cooking in boiling water for 5 minutes.

Alternatively the corn kernels can be stripped from the cob using a knife, and then blanched for 1 minute before bagging-up and freezing.

Tomatoes

Fresh tomatoes will stay in good condition in the fridge for a week or more. Pick when ripe with a deep colour. Green tomatoes make a great chutney, or they can be encouraged to ripen by placing them on a tray in a warm room with a couple of ripe tomatoes or apples. These ripe fruits give off the gas ethylene which will accelerate the ripening of the green fruits.

Freeze The easiest way is just to bung them whole into the freezer. They can easily be skinned after freezing by immersing the frozen tomatoes in hot water for a minute or two, after which the skins will slide off when the fruit is squeezed. Then add to stews etc..

They can also be frozen after stewing to a purée, for use as a base for pasta sauces etc.. Simmer for 5 minutes then sieve before freezing in a plastic container.

Bottle See Part One for methods. First remove the skins of the tomatoes by scalding. Pack tightly and add a teaspoon of salt and a squeeze of lemon juice to each jar. If heating in water, heat to simmering (88°C) in 30 minutes and hold this for a further 50 minutes. If heating in the oven, keep at 150°C for 80 minutes (for up to 2 kg fruit) or for 100 minutes (for up to 5 kg fruit).

Chutney: Green Tomato Chutney

2 kg green tomatoes, 500 g apples, 500 g onions, 250 g raisins, 25 g salt, 500 g sugar, 600 ml vinegar, spices of your choice (e.g. ginger, pepper, chillies)

Finely chop the tomatoes, apples and onions and place all the ingredients in a large pan. Heat gently, stir, and simmer until a pulpy consistency is achieved. Jar up and seal.

Juice

Extract the juice using a fruit press or electric juicer. Freshly-pressed juice will keep only for a day or two in the fridge – but don't forget to freeze some. This can be done in plastic bags inside small boxes (e.g. juice cartons). When frozen, the boxes can be removed and the blocks of juice packed together. Empty plastic milk cartons can also be used for freezing juice, but they must be thoroughly cleaned, and don't forget to leave 5 cm space for expansion as the juice freezes.

Turnips

There are several different varieties of turnips, which can be harvested throughout most times of the year. Like radishes, the roots are only half submerged in the soil and, as they are hardy, can be left there until required. To avoid woodiness, the roots should be pulled before they reach tennis-ball size. Harvested turnips will keep fresh in the fridge for several weeks.

Freeze   Wash, trim and cut into chunks before blanching for 3 minutes. Cool and freeze in plastic bags. To cook from frozen, boil for about 8 minutes.

Dry storage   Pull up in November and gently remove the soil from undamaged roots. Twist off the foliage and pack the roots in sand in boxes. Store in a cool, frost-free building.

Clamp   Rarely used these days, but can be a useful temporary technique for larger quantities. See 'Clamping' in Part One for details.

About the Author

Piers Warren lives in the middle of rural Norfolk where he grows all manner of fruit and vegetables in his garden and polytunnel.

He has had an alarming variety of careers including science teacher, landscape gardener, sound engineer, tree surgeon and multimedia producer! He currently writes on a variety of subjects and works as a conservationist. He is a regular feature writer for a number of magazines including Organic Gardening and Country Smallholding.

Despite all this, he is happiest up to his elbows in compost, or concocting a new chutney recipe in the kitchen. He has always been concerned with environmental issues, and connected with this is his interest in self-sufficiency. He has grown organically for many years, is a vegetarian, and a supporter of permaculture techniques.

His aim is to spend more time tending his smallholding, and less time in front of a computer - although more books are in the pipeline!

Fustyweed

About the Illustrator

Chris Winn is an illustrator and cartoonist. He is neither a gardener nor self-sufficient. He sits in front of a computer most of the day and draws pictures.

As well as being the creator of Mad Gadget, a cartoon strip about a crazy boy inventor which ran in the Young Telegraph for seven years, he is also the author and illustrator of eight books for children and one for adults. The latter, Legal Daisy Spacing, or The Build-A-Planet Manual of Official World Improvements, is a satirical look at the environment, seen from a destructive bureaucrat's point of view. This makes him an unlikely person to illustrate the present book, but you can't have it all ways.

He can be contacted at: chris.winn@paston.co.uk

Also available from Green Books

COMPOSTING FOR ALL
Nicky Scott
with illustrations by Bob Gale

Everyone can compost, whether they have a garden or not. And although more and more people are buying compost bins, they don't always know how to use them properly. This booklet sets out, clearly and simply, all you need to know to ensure success.

The other side of the composting equation is: healthy growth for plants of all shapes and sizes. Why resort to shop-based composts usually made from peat? Leave the peat in the peatbogs where it's supposed to be, and divert all the lovely compostable material away from landfill sites!

Composting for All tells you everything you need for successful home composting, including • beginner's basics • how to mix organic material into a compost heap • worm farming • composting kitchen waste • community projects • heating the heap for fast composting • tips on sieving. Green Books 32pp 216 x 138mm ISBN 1 903998 23 9 £1.95 pb

BACKYARD COMPOSTING
John Roulac

Composting at home reduces your personal volume of rubbish, conserves water, increases plant growth, replaces the need for toxic chemical fertilizers and pesticides, and is also fun. With this little book you can learn how easy it is to • START Discusses all types of composting bins and how to build your own bin from scrap materials • MAINTAIN Includes easy-to-make 'hot recipes', time-saving tips and a troubleshooting chart • USE Save money by making your own free fertiliser at home from leaves, grass and kitchen scraps. Green Books 96pp with photos and line drgs ISBN 1 900322 11 0 £4.95 pb

FOREST GARDENING
Robert A de J Hart

Designed to achieve the utmost economy of space and labour, a forest garden is a tiny imitation of a natural forest. Once established, it requires minimal maintenance, and can provide year-round produce of herbs, fruit and nuts, and root and perennial vegetables. Includes guidelines on designing and maintaining a forest garden, and recommended species for temperate, tropical and sub-tropical climates. Green Books 224pp with 8 colour plates and 20 line drawings 234 x 156mm ISBN 1 900322 02 1 £10.95 pb

Also available from Green Books

GAIA'S GARDEN
A Guide to Home-Scale Permaculture
Toby Hemenway

Permaculture is a verbal marriage of 'permanent' and 'agriculture', pioneered by Bill Mollison. Key features include the use of compatible perennials, non-invasive planting techniques, biodiversity, specific adaptations to local climate, landscape and soil conditions, and highly productive output of edibles. In this low maintenance system, plants are grouped in natural communities, where each species plays a role in building soil, deterring pests, storing nutrients and luring beneficial insects. Chelsea Green (USA) 260pp 252 x 210mm ISBN 1 890132 52 7 £19.95 pb

SEED TO SEED 2nd edition
Seed Saving Techniques for the Vegetable Gardener
Suzanne Ashworth

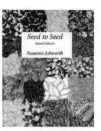

A complete seed-saving guide that describes specific techniques for saving the seeds of 160 different vegetables. For each vegetable it gives botanical classification, flower structure and means of pollination, required population size, isolation distance, techniques for caging or hand-pollination, and also the proper methods for harvesting, drying, cleaning, and storing the seeds. Chelsea Green (USA) 250 x 205mm 320pp 80 b/w photos, resource list, glossary, bibliog. ISBN 1 882424 58 1 £18.95 pb

STRAIGHT-AHEAD ORGANIC
Shepherd Ogden

Intended for the amateur enthusiast who is poised to make the leap to organics, this new edition includes • Garden Siting and Design • Tools and Equipment • Soil and Stability • Food for the Garden (manure and compost) • Garden Planning. Additional chapters cover seeds, setting transplants, irrigation, pests, diseases, and individual vegetables. Chelsea Green (USA) 250 pp 255 x 155mm 100 b&w photos ISBN 1 890132 20 9 £16.95 pb

Also available from Green Books

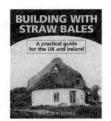